Hymns
for Morning and Evening
Prayer

Hymns
for Morning and Evening
Prayer

Aelred-Seton Shanley

LITURGY
TRAINING
PUBLICATIONS

About the Author

Brother Aelred-Seton Shanley is a lay Benedictine monk and an oblate of the Camaldolese Benedictine community of New Camaldoli in Big Sur, California. While a student in England, he was introduced to monastic life at Quarr Abbey. In 1969, his interest in the emerging vernacular monastic liturgy and a community life more fully engaged with contemporary culture drew him to the community of Mount Saviour Monastery in Elmira, New York. Five years later he began living as a solitary, offering hospitality to guests. In 1982, Archbishop John Francis Whealon of Hartford granted approbation to his life and ministry. Brother Aelred has designed and built the Hermitage of the Dayspring in the hills of northwest Connecticut, a place of monastic worship and hospitality. The Liturgy of the Hours is sung here daily in simple chant settings.

Gabe Huck was the editor of this volume. He was assisted by Audrey Novak Riley and Peter Mazar. The design is by Lucy Smith; the art by Julie Paschkis. Jim Mellody-Pizzato was the production artist; the text is set in Minion, Eras and Papyrus. The printing was done in Toronto, Canada, by Webcom Limited.

Hymn texts © 1999, Aelred-Seton Shanley

HYMNS FOR MORNING AND EVENING PRAYER © 1999, Archdiocese of Chicago: Liturgy Training Publications, 1800 North Hermitage Avenue, Chicago IL 60622-1101; 1-800-933-1800; fax 1-800-933-7094; orders@ltp.org; www.ltp.org. All rights reserved. For reprint information, contact Gabriela Ruelas (fax 1-733-486-7094; e-mail gruelas@ltp.org).

ISBN 1-56854-251-8

HYMNS

$12.00

Contents

Introduction   viii

Christmas Season

Lent

Holy Triduum

Easter Season

Night Prayer

Introduction
Hymns for Rumination

The hymns offered here represent more than twenty-five years of labor and celebration within the Divine Office. They draw on the great themes of the Eastern and Western churches, but also — and perhaps as importantly — on the theological and biblical insights of our times. This collection of hymnodic poems is for all who sing the liturgical Hours in community or who pray them alone — for all, that is, who desire to share deeply in Christ's paschal mystery throughout the liturgical year by celebrating the church's Liturgy of the Hours.

The Office Hymn

The hymns in this collection — a selection from a larger cycle — are my attempt to fill a void that was created when the Liturgy of the Hours was translated into the vernacular. The Second Vatican Council desired that the church's liturgy plumb more deeply the riches of sacred scripture. From this desire there flowered new scripturally based songs for the parish assembly, but these popular songs have not filled the vacuum left by the loss of the ancient Latin *theopoetic* hymns of the Divine Office — that great symphony of daily and sea-sonal praise that Saint Benedict called *opus Dei,* the "work of God."

In the Latin West, the office hymn has come down to us from Saint Ambrose in the fourth century, and others who followed, as one of the few non-scriptural texts in the Liturgy of the Hours (others are the intercessions and collects). In the Eastern churches, hymns and other poetic compositions predominate in the liturgy and form a mosaic of reflection on sacred scripture. In the Western tradition, however, the hymn has held a unique position alongside scripture texts, psalms and canticles from scripture, and scriptural antiphons and responses.

Typology

Through most of the church's history, Christians have delighted in a fluid and imaginative interplay among the scripture stories and images. This interplay, which we call "typology," constantly saw in the scriptures "types" or graphic images that mirrored one another. Thus Israel's Exodus through the Red Sea is seen as a "type" of the homecoming of the Jewish people following their exile in Babylon and also of the Christian's liberation through baptism. The sense is not that these events are over with, but that we participate in these stories here and now within the liturgical *hodie,* the mystical "today" of the liturgical year.

One of the difficulties we face today in our liturgical prayer is an erosion of the foundation on which the poetry of the liturgy was built. If we do not know the scriptures, can we appreciate the scriptural typology, the wonderful play of images in these hymns of the Hours?

These hymns were not composed to transmit information: Within a community already versed in the scriptures, the hymns are catalysts, invitations for God's people, who knew the scriptures as their own story, to grin broadly in enjoyment and thanksgiving.

The great hymns of the patristic period were permeated with this sensibility. *Ad cenam Agni providi,* a seventh-century Latin hymn of the Easter season, provides an example. The poet weaves allusions to the Exodus of Israel's liberation and the liturgical experience of the newly baptized at the Easter Vigil — and, indeed, the experience of the very assembly singing the hymn.

> *Ad cenam Agni providi*
> *Et stolis albis candidi,*
> *Post transitum maris Rubri,*
> *Christo canamus Principi.*

A literal translation would be: "At the supper of the Lamb, clothed in shining white robes after crossing the Red Sea, let us sing to Christ our monarch."

Believers over the centuries have read "between the lines" of this verse and recognized themselves: They too crossed the Red Sea — in their baptism into Christ and indeed their whole lives as baptized persons. They too are clothed in shining robes — the garments of the neophytes. They are summoned to the royal banquet of the Lamb — the Easter eucharist whereby the manna of Israel's desert sojourn becomes one with the church's eucharistic meal. They sing to Christ the Lamb whose blood becomes the sign that frees them from death's angel, the new Moses who leads them into freedom. (See Matthew Britt's *Hymns of the Breviary and Missal,* Benziger, 1922.)

Such fluid and imaginative allusions no longer come easily to many Christians, and these great hymns, usually known only in translations employing the rhyming conventions of the Victorian era, consequently can seem alien. The few relics of office hymns in contemporary hymnals not only suffer in translation, but the ancient chant melodies most often have been replaced by eighteenth- and nineteenth-century foursquare tunes ("At the Lamb's high feast" is most often sung to the tune SALZBURG), and the "new" melody then becomes the medium *and* the message, "reinterpreting" the text.

The Mystical Imagination

Another roadblock to our appreciation of the language of office hymns is that we often take everything literally. In his *Christ in the Early Christian Hymns* (Paulist, 1998), Daniel Liderbach writes: "The less subtle, more empirical, twentieth-century communities of American believers might tend to select only hymns that confess one identity. There is in modern, Western communities the pragmatic value of reducing ambiguity to clarity. Contemporary Americans assume that, even if an occurrence appears to elude rational analysis, it needs to be presented in clear and distinct categories."

William Blake captures well the contrast between "rational analysis" and the mystical imagination. He writes: "When the sun rises, do you not see a round disc of fire, somewhat like a guinea? Oh, no, no, I see an innumerable company of the heavenly host crying 'Holy, Holy, Holy is the Lord God Almighty!' "

Wednesdays may be Wednesdays in the workaday world: the moon and stars simply the moon and stars. But in the Ambrosian hymns of Evening Prayer, steeped in a kind of "sacred play" that makes use of imagery from the cosmology of the book of Genesis, Wednesday is the Fourth Day, the day God creates the moon and stars — and sees that they are good. In such a frame of reference our weekdays take on new significance, giving the days sacrality, coloring and personality.

Gravity

Before the reform of the Office and its translation into the vernacular, certain Latin hymns were sung for days on end: *Christe redemptor omnium* at Christmas, *Ad cenam Agni providi* during the Easter season. The texts offered nourishment worth ruminating upon at length. The texts had "weight" — *gravitas*. Like the liturgy itself, worthy and substantive liturgical hymnody is intended as a vehicle of Christian formation, in Pope John Paul II's words, a "school of sensitivity." Francis Schussler Fiorenza writes: "Hymnic discourse not only addresses God but also expresses personal and com-munitarian sentiments. It not only refers to objective actions, but it utters subjective dispositions. In giving thanks, in praising, and in supplicating, the commu nity manifests something about its own state of existence, so that these acts are in a sense self-transformative." (*Foundational Theology*, Crossroad, 1984)

Many of the verses in our popular hymnals emerged from the churches of the Reformation and from the great current of pietism that informed much hymnody from the seventeenth century onward. The tone of such verse can be described as "private" and "reformative" — I am the sinner Jesus saved. The much-loved hymn "Amazing grace" is an example. The emphasis is on the individual and not on the entire people. The great themes of the liturgical year, its "types" drawn from the scriptures that the fathers and mothers of the church so lovingly and often playfully developed, seldom ring out in such hymns.

Yet these themes continue to challenge us with their transformative vision — a vision of the *already* and the *not yet*, held in tension. In the liturgy we are constantly called to move in time — *backward* to the saving deeds recounted in the oral histories of our scriptures, *forward* toward that day when God is "all in all" — while we march in the here and now, *rehearsing* what is not yet.

Like the liturgy itself, over time a great liturgical hymn transfigures the assembly, enabling it to reflect more and more what Saint Paul called the "mystery of Christ-in-us."

Paradox • One source of the "gravity" of office hymns is their ability to express paradox. Daniel Liderbach speaks of these hymns as employing a "tensive dialectic." By this he means that the mystery of Christ is rich in paradox and that the poet needs to respect the tension that tugs back and forth within the paradox.

Liderbach points out that the great ecumenical councils, grappling with popular understandings of who Jesus is for the church, struggled to articulate not a well-formed Christology but paradox: Jesus is fully human — but Jesus is fully God. The second person of the Trinity is pre-existent — yet born of Mary in historical time. The Word whose power holds all things in being — is self-emptied even unto death.

We are not at ease with ambiguity and paradox. But this is the express genius of the great hymns of the Hours: They hold opposing images in tension.

Kenosis, Agape, Theosis • If a single overarching theme emerges within the hymns in this present collection (reflecting, as I hope they do, their Latin, Greek and Syrian counterparts) it will be the all-embracing self-emptying — *kenosis* — of the Word-made-flesh, who reveals the compassionate love — *agape* — of the Trinity. This theme is of foundational

importance to our faith communities. God embraces
our humanity and wants to draw us continually
and ever more deeply into the fullness of the divine
and triune life — *theosis*.

In the words of Sebastian Moore, "God is interested
in so much more than our recovery." The liturgical
year with its cycles and seasons is a monumental hymn
on this theme, a sacred, spiraling dance celebrating
the "recapitulation" and divinization of the cosmos
in Christ.

The Language in This Collection of Hymns

The post-conciliar church must attempt to reclaim
all that is life-giving in its patristic legacy, but it must
also let go of some images that spoke powerfully to
an earlier age. The *Dies Irae* comes to mind. The tension
is between honoring such a rich legacy and constantly
probing and testing that which is new. This tension
we cannot escape. I believe the engagement nourishes
us, as I hope these verses will show.

We live in the aftermath of Auschwitz and Hiroshima,
in whose shadows our cherished images of God can
seem more hollow than hallowed. In our own day, how
does the poet speak, for instance, of the feast of the
Transfiguration of the Lord, with its images of brilliant
light and glory, when the feast day is coincident with
the anniversary of the bombing of Hiroshima and its
lethal and blinding light? Certainly these images
demand reflection within the liturgy.

The ancient axiom *lex orandi, lex credendi* — the law
of prayer becomes the law of belief — has never chal-
lenged the church as it does today. Let me suggest that
there are times when a spiritual crisis of sorts occurs
even within the liturgy, when what is manifested in our
liturgical assemblies does not even begin to embody, to
make present, the depth of the church's belief. I don't
believe such movements of the heart should be too easily
dismissed as aridity or boredom. There is a tension
between the vitality of our lived *experience* of life in
Christ and an outmoded *vocabulary* that no longer speaks
to this experience. It is out of this crisis that these
hymns have been forged. I hope they may speak to

our times and to all who celebrate, one with another, our resurrection faith.

The Liturgy of the Hours is not a museum. Like every rite of the church, it requires us to use our hearts and minds and tongues, ablaze and illumined by God's Spirit, to transform it into living prayer, to bring forth and proclaim every facet of God's initiative. By profound paradox, in taking our flesh God requires us to use our experience, our vocabulary, our time-bound images in order to reflect what is inexpressible, in order to tell of what is timeless.

I have made an effort to use inclusive language in these hymns. I do not believe such effort is a passing fad. Our perception of the whole Christ is compromised if we rest content with the male-dominated legacy of language, however old within the church and sanctioned by society. I realize, however, that some will feel that the language employed here is not inclusive enough.

God as Abba • In this collection of hymns the first person of the Trinity is almost never spoken of as "he" and only rarely as "father." However, the Aramaic *Abba* is used frequently. While the word is masculine, its very neglect in liturgical usage may free it from more explicitly patriarchal overtones. Biblical scholarship sees *Abba* as embodying the unique intimacy with which Jesus, as firstborn, addressed the God of Sarah and Abraham, especially after the transforming event of his baptism in the Jordan.

That we should have forsaken in the evolution of the liturgy a name for God that most scholars feel was uniquely cherished by Jesus — and handed on to us by Saint Paul — is ironic. Our tradition gives pride of place to the Johannine emphasis on filial relationship and union. Jesus is not content to respond to some nameless "creator" or "holy power." Especially in an era when we are coming to recognize how deep are the wounds sustained when the fundamental relationship between a child and parent is compromised, such a rich vein of theological insight cannot be discarded. The paternal image of *Abba* can be balanced and complemented by a reappropriation of the rich Hebraic feminine image of *Sophia*.

Ruach, Pneuma, Spiritus • In accord with the Hebrew *Ruach* (spirit, breath, wind), I have chosen to use the Hebrew feminine gender in references to the third person of the Trinity. That the "gender" of the Holy Spirit should be defined at all is problematic at best, but why should we settle for the masculine of the Latin *Spiritus* as normative simply because the Roman Empire — until recently — gave us our Western liturgical language? Defining the Spirit as masculine is unfaithful to the earliest traditions (and languages) of the church. Sebastian Brock, the great authority on Saint Ephraim the Hymnographer and Syriac Christianity, a Christianity informed by Semitic rather than Hellenistic origins, writes that "in the earliest literature up to about AD 400 the Holy Spirit is virtually always treated grammatically as feminine" (in *After Eve,* ed. Janet M. Soskice, Marshall Pickering, 1990).

In his *Commentary on Isaiah,* Saint Jerome writes that no one should be scandalized by references to the Holy Spirit as mother, because the Spirit in Hebrew is feminine, and "in the deity there is no gender" — *in divinitate enim nullus est sexus.*

It is my experience that as one begins to associate God's Spirit with the feminine, as the Hebrew scriptures do, wonderful new vistas open up. Reading Saint Paul or the Fourth Evangelist on the Spirit then profoundly expands one's understanding and appreciation.

Mary, the Mother of God • In the hymns that celebrate Mary, the Mother of God, I have used the Semitic *Myriam* instead of the English "Mary." By using the Semitic form of this holy name I hope we can honor and reclaim Mary's Jewishness, her ancestry as a daughter of Abraham and Sarah. As a faithful Jew, as also the mother of God's Anointed, Myriam the "Bearer of God" — *Theotokos* — stands at the watershed of history. Centuries of Christian devotion and piety, while extolling her holiness, have perhaps too easily divorced her from the family of Israel and forgotten her as a daughter of the Torah. Of course, she is known as Myriam in all the Eastern liturgies of the church.

Musical Settings of the Hymns

The texts offered here have been printed without musical settings. Though the hymns are eminently singable — indeed, I hope they will be reproduced and sung in the heart of the faith community — I hope also that they will first be prayed as lyrical prose-poems, and only then as hymns. To this end these verses have been laid out as a book of poetry.

While the most frequent meter used in this collection is Long Meter (LM) — four lines, each of eight syllables — for which hundreds of melodies are available, other familiar meters also are included.

To assist those who want to sing them, the meter of each hymn has been given with its text, and an appendix provides a small collection of chant tones chosen for their simplicity and ease of singing by an unaccompanied assembly. Beyond these, for an immense variety of suggestions for other melodies, the minister of music need only refer to the metrical index of any of the great hymnals published today. See, for instance, the Episcopal *Hymnal 1982,* the Lutheran *Book of Worship,* GIA's *Hymnal for the Hours* and *Worship.*

The Domesticity of the Office • Unlike our Sunday eucharistic gatherings where we have first to assemble, the Liturgy of the Hours presumes something more domestic: The family of faith, in the midst of its daily rhythms and routines, is simply taking time out, the liturgical equivalent of a morning or afternoon coffee break or a gathering before dinner. These are not usually full meals, and the menu isn't rich or elaborate. It is here that the chant settings of the hymns allow us to "settle in" and catch a breath amid all our busy-ness.

On holidays when we hold a full-scale celebration we often enjoy pulling out all the stops — and we bring energy to the endeavor. On ordinary days, in contrast, our enthusiasm and energy varies from day to day. Most times anything too celebratory will be experienced as forced. Perhaps it was out of such an awareness of the simple joys of ordinary days that most of the ancient hymn tones emerged.

A tension may be at work as we attempt to celebrate the Hours in a parochial setting, especially in parishes where Morning or Evening Prayer is a special event. When the celebration becomes elaborate there is a danger that the natural domesticity of the Hours will be lost.

This domestic quality of the monastic office, its humdrum "seven times a day" quality when celebrated by a settled monastic family, is an invaluable gift and reminder to the church at large.

With our increased desire to "do" liturgy well, there inevitably comes the temptation to "do it up well." In the Divine Office, especially where it is celebrated daily, we should strive toward an economy of form, shorn of excess. The chants of the church's musical heritage, by their very chasteness, call us back to what we profess to be doing, that is, praying *in Christ* to the Holy One before whom words fail.

The hymn at the beginning of the Hours is not meant to accompany sacred action. The form of the office hymn has its own integrity and must speak for itself. Its words must not be overwhelmed by its musical setting. The hymn that opens Morning or Evening Prayer is followed by quiet reflectiveness, the interiority of psalms, canticle and reading.

Old Melodies or New? • The musical settings of the hymns of the monastic office found in the *Antiphonale Monasticum* (Solesmes/Desclée, Tournai, 1934) are one of the most precious musical legacies of Western medieval civilization, occupying a unique place among the world's mystical traditions. Whether the simplest or the most complex, for centuries they have allowed the Christian spirit to soar in song and praise. In the process, many of the most hallowed melodies — Christmas's *Christe redemptor omnium, Crux fidelis* of Passiontide, or *Ad cenam Agni providi* of Easter — have accrued a holiness from prayer-filled use by the assemblies of God's faithful. Even today, in most Benedictine and Cistercian communities, a certain *frisson* can be felt throughout the community on the eve of the Advent season as the cantor intones *Conditor alme siderum.* These melodies have come to carry within them the very spirit of the church's prayer, and they provide a nexus wherein faith, rite, poetry and song converge to give tangible expression to the great mysteries of our salvation.

It is my contention that these ancient tones continue to have life in them and are truly capable of expanding the hearts and minds of those who sing them. The simplest can be sung by the most unschooled assembly and the most complex can be brought to life by a community that loves to sing.

Why would we want to sing these seemingly out-moded melodies, few of which are found in modern hymnals? We live in a musical culture accustomed to "easy listening." Very often the modal music of our forebears in the faith seems austere, especially in contrast to popular music or the sonorities of a film score. Yet austerity is precisely their gift to us. When we gather in our assemblies to sing the Liturgy of the Hours we are being invited to return to the "better part," to come to rest within a chaste melody that is sung antiphonally in the unity of Father, Son and Spirit.

Chant traditionally does not invite instrumental accompaniment and therefore does not depend on it. It is purely the voice's outpouring: "My mouth shall proclaim your praise." This means that even the most musically disadvantaged need not feel abandoned. Years of experience with "un-musical" guest-retreatants have shown me that the most common chant tones of the Gregorian repertoire are accessible to even the smallest group gathered to sing the Divine Office. They offer a depth of feeling that can carry us when a more popular hymn melody simply taxes or overwhelms us.

Popular melodies, with their measured rhythms, their rests, eighths, quarters and whole notes, make greater musical demands on the assembly, and with few exceptions are almost always better served by musical accompaniment. Chant tones are less exacting, and thus they allow the assembly to focus on the text and the integrity of the words. For this reason a collection of Gregorian hymn tones is offered in the appendix in the hope that these may be rediscovered anew by all who desire to sing Morning and Evening Prayer. While the majority of these tones are direct transcriptions in modern notation of their chant counterparts, I have also adapted, simplified or created new tones in the spirit of the old for ease of singing. One of these adaptations will be noticed by those familiar with the chant and the Latin texts. In a number of instances where a tune has two or more notes on a single syllable, I have tried to arrange the groupings to fit well with the accentuation of the English texts. Chant tones for the four Marian antiphons of night prayer are also included in the appendix.

With today's sophisticated word-processing programs one can effectively point the verses of a hymn without resorting to placing each syllable of each verse under the music. Leaving the text as *verse* allows for a deeper assimilation of the meaning. For example: an umlaut or dieresis [¨] can be used to indicate a syllable sung on *two* notes. An italicized syllable indicates that it is sung on *three or more* notes. One underlined character of a syllable indicates it is held.

Embodied Praise

In almost every Christian tradition the hymn is sung standing rather than sitting. In this it models the ancient *orans,* the stance of the friend of God, a friend no longer enslaved but free. And it is precisely because we are able to stand that we are able to *bow* freely, generously, in adoration.

Traditionally the liturgical hymn concludes with a doxology sung in the posture of bowing, and it is at this point that we are invited to bring the whole of ourselves into our praise, not just our voices but our bodies as well. The preceding verses, coming as they usually do at the very start of a celebration, have plunged us into one particular facet of the mystery of "Christ-in-us." In the process we are transformed. When we come to bow, we *are* Christ self-emptied before his Abba.

The deep bow — no matter that it is "un-American" — is common to all the world's religious traditions as a universal sign of abasement, honoring the Other, an abasement not simply out of unworthiness but out of overwhelming reverence and gratitude.

As you sing the hymns offered here, in even the simplest of liturgical settings, open yourselves to the transformative power of such embodied praise. Several doxologies are included on the last page of this book; they can be used when no doxology has been provided in place for any 88.88 hymn.

Acknowledgments

I owe an immense debt of gratitude to the English Benedictine nuns of Stanbrook Abbey who first opened my eyes to the possibility of a new hymnody. To Sister Anne Field, OSB, of Stanbrook, who graciously reviewed many of these verses and made invaluable comments, I am especially indebted. My love of the liturgy and the church's chant and hymns was first nurtured by David Hugh Farmer and Abbot Aelred Sillem, OSB, of the Solesmes Congregation's Abbey of Saint Mary of Quarr in England. The late Eric Routley of Princeton, a great authority on Christian hymnody, offered line-by-line criticism of my early hymns and told me I was on the right track. The monastic community of Mount Saviour, Elmira, New York, offered me my first full experience of a vernacular monastic liturgy, and it was in that community that I first embarked on this labor. I remain grateful for so much I received there, imbued as it was with the spirit of its founder, Father Damasus Winzen. Likewise, I am indebted to my confrere, John Leinenweber, who, with a critical and dispassionate eye, generously helped edit these texts over the years. And finally, without the enthusiasm of Gabe Huck, editor at Liturgy Training Publications, for these texts, and his constant challenge to me to refine and rewrite, these hymns might never have been shared with the broader church.

In very few cases I have taken what some may see as a gross liberty in rewriting another's hymn, or using it as a framework for an entirely new text of my own. A list of these texts is given on page *xxxix*, under "Further Acknowledgments." However, evolving theological insight, contemporary usage, and the unique needs of a *liturgical* hymnody have invited such changes, and I hope in the process I have only climbed on to the shoulders of those whose faith and skill preceded me. A number of these hymns were inspired by English translations of the Latin texts of the *Officium Romanum* by Aelred Squire, OSB, CAM., a much-loved monk of my spiritual community, the Hermitage of New Camaldoli in Big Sur, California. I have freely mined his renderings for the richness of their images. Father Aelred died in 1997.

I am grateful to the Benedictine communities of Mount Saviour, Christ in the Desert, and New Camaldoli who have used many of these texts, in varying degrees of revision, in their liturgy over the years. I offer these hymns as a fellow pilgrim who has grappled with and surrendered to the embrace of God's wrestling angel. May they contribute to the church's sacrifice of praise.

— Brother Aelred-Seton Shanley, OBL, OSB, CAM.

And so it is
we gather here,
love's song
upon our lips
and heart.
We send our voice
upon the winds:
we with
the earth —
God's work of art!

Ordinary Time

O fire that fuels the stars and suns,
rekindled in our evening flame:
your blinding radiance yet is dimmed
before the One from whom you came.

When out of darkness first you dawned,
you ushered in God's gifts untold:
on this the eighth, unequaled day,
you blazed where Life lay dead and cold.

For Christ, our light, unquenchable,
death sought to master and defy,
yet from a darkened, empty tomb
Life gave definitive reply.

The universe will not be shamed,
delighting God in endless ways,
for neither human sin nor pride
can silence its unceasing praise. Amen.

88.88

2

First uttered, first conceived and named
by Love unbounded, unrestrained:
before all else that came to be,
"Light!" dark and silence overcame.

Without this nothing could endure,
yet through it, all life came to be!
Light's energies by God unleashed
would birth each world and galaxy.

Alone, apt symbol for the One
beyond all image and all form:
pervading all, yet uncontained,
of all that God has made, first born.

The fire within the burning bush,
the radiance seen on Moses' face,
the guide that led the magi forth,
Mount Tabor's brilliant, dazzling grace!

"Light!" pulse of everything alive,
from rainbow to the sun's fierce rays,
from fireflies to the farthest star,
you manifest God's hidden ways! Amen.

88.88

3

This is the first day
of the world's creation,
when from deepest silence
Wisdom spoke and stars played —
day, too, of new birth,
in Christ's death and rising,
forming a new earth.

This day the light broke,
called forth out of chaos
by God, Creator,
through the Word that Love spoke;
as with bright-spread wing
Wisdom, warm-breathed, hovered —
life's ground of being.

This is the new day,
raised in Christ beyond time:
gift full of promise,
both the first and eighth day!
Goal of creation —
Alpha as Omega —
Christ its completion.

Throughout our planet
praise wells up to bless you,
Abba, most holy,
with your Word and Spirit,
as at time's dawning,
so through endless ages,
for this new morning! Amen.

11.11.11.5

4

Can we conceive when time was not,
the nothingness of cosmic sleep?
When, formless, there was only void:
no near, no far, no height, no deep?

In love's embrace, God's uttered Word
then sounded from Life's boundless heart:
like suns exploding into space,
"Light!" burst forth, dazzling, in the dark.

Upon the deep there spread delight
for God had smiled, and deemed it "good!"
Like solar winds was Wisdom's breath,
her warmth yet gentle on her brood.

Dividing light from darkness, then
God called light "Day!" and darkness "Night!"
Thus ev'ning came and morning came —
this first of days and God's delight. Amen.

88.88

5

Dawn's radiance washes over earth,
refreshed and rested from the night:
the grateful world, awake, aware
is bathed in Christ's baptismal light.

Emblazoned thus, our earth proclaims
its first foundation and its end.
Another day stirs life afresh:
its gifts from God to God all tend.

O Christ, indwelling source of life,
reflecting fair your Abba's face,
your radiance brightens all the earth
as we awake in your embrace.

Within your love we sing our praise,
transcendent God who nurture all;
day's dawning splendor sends us forth
to answer with our lives your call. Amen.

88.88

6

The blazing energies of light,
unleashed when God said "Let it be,"
in fusion formed the womb of life,
the rain clouds and the raging sea.

These parted, each to its domain,
divided by the vault of sky;
untamed and turbulent, unchecked,
within them life and death would vie.

Those waters clothed our planet home,
so terrible and yet so fair:
the gift without which all would cease,
yet placed, so fragile, in our care.

Both sign and sacrament of life,
of love awash, poured out and fresh:
engulfing all that sin would spawn,
while nurt'ring life in all the rest.

Thus evening came and morning came
that second day when waters burst:
both flood and freshness for our world,
chaste herald of our second birth. Amen.

88.88

The waters of our mother earth,
her rivers, oceans, lakes and springs,
are mirrors to the depths of God —
the freshness at the heart of things.

Our sister water, wondrous gift,
can cleanse and cool, destroy and drown:
the mistress of both life and death,
through her all living things are bound.

For Noah she was fearsome flood
whose rage not even God foresaw.
For Naaman, seeking miracles,
her modesty was cause for awe.

Her currents held the Lord of life,
abyss of death, baptismal tomb.
With blood she came forth from his side
as breaking waters from the womb.

O Christ in whom we are baptized,
washed clean, refreshed, and sanctified:
be praised for this our sister fair
by whom we live, in whom we died. Amen.

88.88

8

O sister dawn, how light your touch;
how bright your face upon the earth!
Awakened are we all to life
as you call us from sleep's small death.

You, sister, graced that Easter morn
when Life, entombed, was lost from sight.
You roused the women with their spice
and guided them to greet the Light!

Your dawning opens wide our eyes;
our talents are awakened, too!
Our hands, so grasping, rest has freed
to welcome gifts we never knew.

Aroused, awakened and aware,
hands turn to labor, hearts to pray:
what yesterday was only glimpsed
stands now as fresh and clear as day.

With dawn and all the gifts of day,
we praise you, Abba, Breath and Word:
a world so prodigal and free
reveals your loving hand, O God! Amen.

88.88

Life, never bounded or constrained,
tamed chaos, took the floods in hand,
determined these should now recede
and bare what would become the land.

And so, this day, their bound'ries set,
God named one "Earth!" the other "Sea!"
And then, beholding both were good,
Love's eye was drawn to shrub and tree.

Life thus addressed our mother earth,
and charged her: Color, bloom and root!
Be lavish in the gifts you bear
of greening forests, plants and fruit!

And so it was and it was good!
Our planet's splendors stood untrod;
each peak, each valley, plain and pond
poured forth its poetry to God.

Thus evening came and morning came
the third day, when our earth first breathed;
so fragile, faithful, fruitful, free:
by Life sustained, by Love conceived! Amen.

88.88

10

How blest you trees that mantle earth,
you leafy crown upon our world,
who hold your limbs in ceaseless praise,
whose canopy our God unfurled.

The wonder of this holy gift
whose leaves renew our atmosphere,
providing shelter, tools and shade,
whose fruits so gen'rously you share.

Apt symbol: supple, bending, strong,
your roots plunged deep and limbs held high,
self-healing, ever branching-out,
still giving even when you die.

From time primordial you stood,
both pole and axis — sacred tree:
mute witness to our joy and shame
in Eden as on Calvary.

Your limbs embraced the Lord in death
when, fearful, each disciple fled;
your branches leafed in joy's excess
to see Christ risen from the dead. Amen.

88.88

Where stretch the limits of the stars?
Who fathoms all the gifts of earth?
Within the origins of life
one Word, in labor, gives them birth.

11

Its silence fills the stellar night;
its sound plumbs deep our planet's core:
poured out for us, enfleshed in full,
this Word — none other — Mary bore.

From earth, the Word drew nourishment,
from us, the body we possess;
our sun provided warmth and light —
with these the Word took on our flesh.

All things created, great and small,
at dawn of time God sanctified:
now these, enfleshed within the Word,
return God's love, thus glorified.

For only thus the Word prepared
to consummate the sacrifice
for which God's heart had ever yearned,
for which Love would alone suffice.

Creation's dawning God deemed "Good!"
yet still we scarce believe our worth:
but pregnant, full, the Word here dawns,
and yearns in us to come to birth. Amen.

88.88

12

There was no sun to rule the day,
no moon to roam the night until
our God flung forth the nebulae,
the planets, suns and stars at will.

With these God made the greater light
to dawn and blaze upon our day;
a lesser lamp illumined night
and marked each month along its way.

Thus time, the seasons and the years
began their endless ordered round;
the moon called forth the festivals
on which God's praises would resound.

And so it was and it was good!
Companions, friends, the stars would be:
bright beacons in the cosmic night,
sure bearings both on land and sea.

Thus evening came and morning came.
The fourth day saw our day-star, sun,
bright symbol of undying light,
undimmed when day and night are done. Amen.

88.88

13

O searing splendor, brother sun,
whose beams enfold our planet-home,
whose energies sustain all life:
surpassing all but God alone!

And you, our lovely sister moon,
who tend the tides, the months define;
your waxing beauty kindles hope
and leaves night gentler when you shine.

Be blest, O God, for father sky,
for all within our Milky Way:
by night a tapestry of light,
a boundless vault of blue by day.

Each stone, each solitary star,
each creature drawing breath from earth,
reverberates with grace within,
revealing your creative mirth. Amen.

88.88

14

Still dim, a fresh new world now dawns
as dark departs before the day.
Night by our day-star is deposed
'til brother sun has had his say.

The moon, the stars, the earth and sun
sing out their sacrificial praise,
and bend their brilliance to that light
which sets all other lights ablaze!

As day and night to each give way,
they herald Christ's self-offering,
whose eucharist embraces all,
whose holiness fills ev'ry thing.

Here is the triune sacrifice:
God's Love, by Love, in Love outpoured!
The cosmos is by Christ espoused:
in earth's embrace God is adored. Amen.

88.88

God's glory, Christ, our new-dawned day, 15
in deep compassion for our earth,
has raised what we had left for dead,
and healed what sin had scarred at birth.

The Alpha and Omega, Christ,
today and yesterday: the same!
who manifests the great unseen:
who by the nameless One is named!

Word of God's silence, sounding still
beneath the surface of each day;
both cloud by day and flame by night,
companion, goal, our guide and way.

We bless you, Abba, brimming love,
and Christ, your well-beloved Son,
who with your Spirit breathe in us:
three-personed yet for ever one. Amen.

88.88

16

Our mother earth, her mantle green,
lay ripened, seeded and at rest;
she yearned to nurture all to life,
providing nourishment and nest.

So God, unbounded, uncontained,
ordained the oceans teem with life
and bid the skies be filled with flight:
with fish and fowl the world was rife.

These each were blest and both deemed good!
God urged them mate and multiply:
thus life would ever be increased
and God in all be glorified.

With song and plumage, soaring flight,
birds blazoned forth God's gifts so free;
while sea-life, fathomless and feared,
reflected, dark, God's mystery.

Thus evening came and morning came
the fifth day, filling air and sea.
Life overflowing and outpoured
depends upon diversity! Amen.

88.88

Be praised, O God, for fish and fowl,
in species past imagining:
diverse and myriad in form,
each fitted fair with fin or wing.

With dawn and dusk in tuneful praise
their song cascades throughout the air:
these wingéd messengers of joy
proclaim your providence and care.

The dove was herald of your truce,
an olive branch its sign of peace;
the raven brought Elijah bread;
at cockcrow Peter's lying ceased.

When Jonah turned his back and fled,
his wayward course a whale reversed;
to Peter, hauling in his catch,
you showed just how diverse your church.

We bless these creatures of the sea,
these feathered couriers of your grace,
who show us in their play and flight
the trust that comes with your embrace. Amen.

88.88

18

Lord, lover of the human heart,
earth's source, her dawn, her day and rest:
how holy is our planet-home,
whose gifts your love all manifest.

So deep your love, so reckless, sure,
you loved us even in our sin:
pursued us, shared our pain and death,
determined at the last to win!

Embrace, enfold us in your breath;
so warmed, may we be set ablaze.
Close draw us to your wounded side —
the wounds we bear will then be grace.

Love, crucified, twice hallows earth,
which God deemed good and filled with grace:
here, holy ground; here, heaven's gate;
with awe therefore our earth embrace!

We bless you, holy, deathless One!
We bless you, Christ, God's wounded Word!
We bless you, Breath, our breath and life;
your praise through all the earth be heard! Amen.

88.88

The fields and plains were still ungrazed,
the ground untouched by things that crawl,
when God called creatures forth to play,
and wondrously earth bore them all.

Then Life, beholding all was good,
in overflowing joy conceived:
"Let us now human beings make!"
God gave them breath that Sabbath eve.

"Let them, together and alone,
our image be, our likeness bear.
To you I give your kin the beasts
and all the earth into your care.

"For she has borne all living things;
her fruits will give you nourishment.
As for the flocks and herds, let them
with grass and foliage be content."

Thus evening came and morning came,
the sixth day, giving God delight,
for everything was very good,
one with another ordered right!

The earth, God saw, was now complete —
a marvel of diversity!
So mirrors earth its Maker's life,
revealed within the Trinity. Amen.

88.88

20   Our God be praised for peopling earth
with life upon our planet-home:
you called four-leggeds forth to range,
to multiply and freely roam.

Our kin, these beasts, the herds and flocks
have grazed in vast diversity;
one each with earth, they knew her ways
in union, not adversity.

Beholding such variety,
Love's heart had leapt at what could be:
a creature who, once loved, could love,
who with the eyes of God could see.

With these the Holy One would share
what Wisdom boldly had conceived;
with these our earth would find a voice
to sing of all she had received.

And so it is we gather here,
love's song upon our lips and heart.
We send our voice upon the winds:
we with the earth — God's work of art! Amen.

88.88

21

Creator of this dawning day,
creation finds its rest in you:
though all must change and taste decay,
you touch our hearts and they are new!

We bless you, Abba, for this earth,
for all the wonder it retains.
Though we may spurn you in our sin,
your selfless gift of love remains.

Touched by this gift may mind and heart
your praise throughout the world proclaim,
and may this love deep in our hearts
set others blazing with its flame.

The seventh day, this day of rest,
you call us to rehearse your reign:
to cease from work and with delight
to rev'rence all that you sustain.

Most blessed Trinity of love,
for whom the human heart was made,
to you be praise in ceaseless song
on this our Sabbath, blessed day! Amen.

88.88

22 Strong God, the beam and ground of things,
fixed course, their hub and permanence;
the fire at the heart of earth,
day's promise and its radiance!

Your word form ev'ry word we tongue;
our hearts keep focused, chaste and free.
Uncloud our sight to gaze with love,
then we shall know true liberty.

Be light to us when day is done
and tend us, vuln'rable, in sleep.
Death holds no fear where you are all:
day's labors done, your rest we reap. Amen.

88.88

O true dominion, God, at play
within the flux of sun and moon;
you spark the flint of morning light,
then sear the world at pitch of noon.

Clasp in your own our hands, so clenched,
that rail at love, then flirt with sin:
make strong our limbs, heal mind and heart;
like springs, your peace well up within.

Let intellect and voice and strength
be drum and cymbal of your praise:
the dying embers of our love
fan bright till we are set ablaze. Amen.

88.88

24 Lord God, whose breath all being breathes,
outpoured, self-emptied, shared in Christ:
our restless hearts seek rest in you
who counted not love's awful price.

How boundless is this love you bear
to share the anguish of our sin,
to suffer at our hands the cross
that life might trample death and win!

Our joy, indeed our very life
is hidden now within your heart:
such is the wonder of the gift
we harvest-in till day is dark. Amen.

88.88

You
angel choirs,
now mark the day:
prepare a new song
for our earth.
God comes,
self-stripped
of majesty to die;
but dying,
gives us birth!

A d v e n t

O radiance, Christ, O joyous light,
whose mirth brings all the stars to birth:
our Abba's fullness far outpoured
beyond the fragile hopes of earth.

Word sounding in creation's core,
embodied in a maiden's heart,
received in wonder: wonderful
God's Word-made-flesh within this ark.

Your great compassion knew no bounds
to save us from the brink of hell.
You'd come, espoused, through Mary's womb:
Life, sacrificed, to make us well.

Night weighed upon our war-torn world
when silently you pitched your tent.
Front-runner, bridegroom, blazing sun,
to claim the prize your sole intent.

How glorious your victory!
Your name alone the name we bear.
Come judge the living and the dead,
yet pity us whose flesh you share. Amen.

88.88

25

26

God's word which sounds throughout the world,
whose mercy wraps us round and round,
in John now finds an urgent voice:
"Repent! God's grace shall here abound!"

Relentless as the searing sun
yet gentle as the morning dew,
this voice cries in our wilderness:
"Receive the Gift; be born anew!"

The broken reed will Christ restore,
frail flames he'll fan to blazing fire;
with tenderness our wounds he'll bind,
the flock he shepherds, saved entire.

Anointed with the Spirit's pow'r,
he'll preach good news, make strong the weak,
demanding justice for the poor,
the basic rights that all would seek.

Our eyes, so blind, will see God's reign
revealed in those we once ignored;
our tongues that babble, gossip, rage
will speak out for the voiceless poor.

Lord Jesus, come: find us awake,
rehearsing now what is not yet.
This work of God, our works of God,
your glorious coming manifest! Amen.

88.88

O Myriam, prepare the day
when God takes shelter at your breast;
the Word, creation's source and end,
now with our features will take flesh.

The wedding chamber of your womb —
expectant, hallowed, fenced around —
grows full, so heavy now with child
whose name, "God heals," through earth will sound.

This Word, though birthless, comes to birth,
whose day the prophets strained to see.
Compassion, justice now embrace
and bare God's great fidelity.

You angel choirs, now mark the day:
prepare a new song for our earth.
God comes, self-stripped of majesty
to die; but dying, gives us birth! Amen.

88.88

28

The prophets weave their mounting fugue:
"God's own anointed one is near!"
True justice, ever sought on earth,
from tender bud will soon appear.

God comes to birth, in flesh, to heal —
a shepherd seeking out the stray —
to bind our wounds, to lift us up,
and ever more keep death at bay.

A second birth we also sing:
Christ knocks and waits for our reply.
He yearns to sit us down and serve
the feast of God's unbounded joy.

O earth, prepare your manger-cave;
you heavens, Glorias rehearse;
our race its Virgin-mother boasts:
prepare, each one, our Savior's birth! Amen.

88.88

29

Come, lovely Lord, outdazzle day;
come clear our clouded sight to see
your coming deep in every deed,
in labor's love, eternity!

Come nurture what your hand has made;
come bring to term what you have sown.
In all creation Christ be seen:
the seed and sum of all we own.

Come, Sov'reign, in your simple gifts,
come seal us in integrity.
Your birth in flesh once wedded earth:
come now in new nativity! Amen.

88.88

From east
to west,
from shore
to shore,
let all the earth
awake and sing!
Adore the child
whom Mary bore,
an infant,
yet our Lord
and King.

30

O Christ, in whom all is redeemed,
who shone before created light:
sprung from our Abba's boundless heart,
by God begotten, God's delight!

Be mindful, Savior of our world,
you once were bound in swaddling bands,
and from a maiden's hallowed womb
you gave yourself into our hands.

The stars themselves shine bright as suns;
creation at its core is changed:
a wondrous new song fills the night,
the galaxies cannot contain!

With hearts made whole within your love,
we join this song of ransomed earth,
whose healing through your cross began
this hallowed night that saw your birth.

Most holy, moth'ring, fath'ring God,
be praised in Christ, your heart's delight:
come now in new nativity
and find your joy in us this night. Amen.

88.88

31

This night when winter's darkness deep
dares hope to dawn within its heart,
when all is plunged in deepest sleep,
the stillness sounds with angels' art.

The stars themselves take up the song
of him who knows our fragile worth.
This night God's love is manifest,
self-emptied, cradled, come to birth!

Such awesome love demands our all;
our earth can never be the same.
Our frail humanity was freed
when God this night so gently came.

Can we begin to comprehend
this myst'ry nursing Mary's breast,
which challenges our human hopes,
and never more will let us rest?

Our God whom likenesses elude
has yet this night emblazoned earth
with this one image of Love's heart:
an infant, vuln'rable from birth.

O Abba, fath'ring forth this gift,
O Spirit, nourishing this child,
we bow in deep, adoring praise:
this night the world is reconciled! Amen.

88.88

32

From east to west, from shore to shore,
let all the earth awake and sing!
Adore the child whom Mary bore,
an infant, yet our Lord and King.

Behold, the world's creator wears
the form and fashion of a slave;
our very flesh our maker shares,
that none be lost and all be saved.

How wond'rous this, the work God wrought:
a virgin's womb, God's dwelling place!
Beyond the bounds of should and ought
her "Yes" now floods the world with grace.

The One on whom bright angels gaze
is warmed by cattle from the herd.
On wood, warm-nestled in some straw,
is laid God's uncreated Word.

The angels' chorus fills the air
and echoes through the silent fields.
Alone, unlettered shepherds see
the shepherd-God their song reveals.

God's glory, Christ, O Virgin-born,
is yours from all eternity.
Accept our praise this blessed morn,
O love outpoured, O Trinity! Amen.

88.88

33

Christ is here, Emmanuel!
Majesty so mild:
Wisdom dwells with grace and truth,
hidden in this child.

Born of God's creative will,
Christ is light from light,
come to rescue Adam's race
waiting in the night.

(December 26: St. Stephen)
Great the myst'ry here revealed:
God known in this child!
Stephen, stoned to death, proclaims
all things reconciled.

(December 27: St. John)
Great the myst'ry here revealed:
wide is God's embrace!
To this one command of love
John gives pride of place.

(December 28: Holy Innocents)
Great the myst'ry here revealed:
violence sees increase;
innocents, though slain, shall live:
theirs the Prince of Peace.

Abba, Word and Spirit, One,
earth and heaven sing:
all creation with one voice
praise and worship bring! Amen.

75.75

The root of Jesse now has flow'red,
for Sarah's daughter bears a son!
Behold, the Mother of our God
draws to her breast the Holy One.

The co-eternal Word of God
is cradled now in slumber deep:
he who holds planets to their course
now nestles in her arms, asleep.

The law which girds the universe,
God's Torah teaching Wisdom's ways,
in Mary, both have been enfleshed —
a source of scandal and God's praise.

This Jewish daughter's bold consent,
her wonderment, her "Let it be!"
has touched the very depths of God
and ever changed the way we see.

A contradiction to our time,
her single "Yes!" to what could be.
Have we such openness within
to bring the Word to birth as she? Amen.

88.88

35 Hail Myriam, most holy Wisdom's child,
you model all we hope and yearn to be.
You are the crown of gen'rous womanhood;
in you there dawns a new humanity!

The paradise that Eve, our sister, left
returns to us in you a hundredfold.
The child you bore has opened heaven's doors
and gathers all who stray into his fold.

O gate through which such royal progress goes,
O beacon guiding all upon their way,
behold how peoples ev'rywhere, redeemed,
have blessed the fruit your womb has borne this day!

O Jesus, born so fair of Mary's flesh,
she carried you to term, nine months, content:
be praised for this, God's boundless love for earth,
which drew our sister's bold and blest consent! Amen.

10.10.10.10

36

Gift-laden magi make their way
to One whose gift surpasses all:
our Abba's fullness here outpoured,
now nestled in a cattle-stall.

Gold long had gilt the courts of kings
and incense gave the gods delight,
but myrrh was bitter, deemed for death,
and shed on these a diff'rent light.

Unschooled, mere shepherds see this birth,
not priests so learned in the law;
now magi come, uncircumcised,
to worship on a stable floor.

Creation's very core is changed:
the Lord of all, baptized, bends low
and, plunging into Jordan's depths,
comes up with earth renewed in tow!

The commonplace is charged with life!
A marriage feast becomes a sign:
God weds our earth, a cherished bride,
while changing water into wine.

O God whose gifts are manifest
in ways beyond imagining:
O Abba, Word and Spirit-breath,
with joy your boundless love we sing! Amen.

88.88

37

Famed though the world's great cities be,
yet none can Bethlehem excel,
for now there dawns God's deathless day
on Gentiles as on Israel.

More dazzling than the dawning sun,
this star that blazes at Christ's birth
proclaims to all the waiting world:
our God enfleshed upon this earth.

They who have listened to earth's ways,
who long have studied heaven's stars,
come seeking Wisdom's holy source —
their route a different one from ours.

Prostrate before the throne of grace,
they offer gifts both choice and rare:
gifts God first gave our mother earth,
her gold, her frankincense and myrrh.

Earth's sacred gifts speak mysteries:
incense God's holiness extolled,
God's sovereign realm the gold proclaimed,
but myrrh the cross and death foretold.

The magi, finding all they sought,
then traveled home a different way;
for nothing now remained the same
in light of what they found this day. Amen.

88.88

All praise to you, O Lord,
who heard your mother's plea,
and manifest your glory first
at Cana's wedding feast.

You speak, and it is done;
obedient to your word,
the water blushing into wine
proclaims you as its Lord.

May new life now be ours,
in you to ever live;
may we drink of that sourceless stream
which you alone can give.

So, led from strength to strength,
grant us, O Christ, to see
the wedding supper of the Lamb,
God's great epiphany! Amen.

88.88

Let us receive
these lenten days
with joy,
recalling Eve
and Adam's
broken fast —
the fruit which
parted us
from Paradise
but left us longing
to return at last.

Lent

Fear not! I am the first and last,
I am the Lord, the living one;
as I lay down my life, alone,
I'll take it up when death's undone.

39

Was Christ not bound to suffer so
before his glory was revealed?
His chastisement has made us whole
and by his scourging we are healed.

God's will it was that Christ be bruised,
his life a sacrifice unstained.
May he who bears such glorious wounds
guard and preserve us as he reigns.

Baptized into this death of his,
we also hope to live in him.
If we endure, his reign is ours;
upon his cross is nailed our sin.

Christ yesterday and Christ today!
All things' beginning and their end!
The Alpha and Omega now,
toward whom the course of ages tends. Amen.

88.88

40 O Lord, in whom this day first dawned,
who clothe creation wondrously,
that you should clothe yourself in flesh
is yet more wonderful to see!

Then follows the proper verse for each Sunday of Lent from the normative
Year A gospels, followed by the concluding verses below.

First Sunday

We cannot live by bread alone,
you taught us in the wilderness:
each word that comes from God most high
is lenten fare and feast for us.

Second Sunday

Transfigured on Mount Tabor's height,
creation's glory was unveiled,
and yet your cross alone would show
the awful price that this entailed.

Third Sunday

You cried "I thirst" upon the cross
in anguish that our hearts be healed;
within us living waters spring:
life in its fullness is revealed!

Fourth Sunday

You braved the depths of all despair
to lead us forth to day's delight:
our blindness you dispelled by faith;
we are illumined in your light.

"O Lazarus," you cried, "Come forth!"
This death seemed more than you could bear;
but death had not the final say:
life in its fullness you would share.

In nature one with God, First-born,
you never claimed your rightful due,
but bore our emptiness and pain
in serving those whose wounds you knew.

Now raised to heights where names all fail,
proclaimed "The Lord," O risen Christ,
in you alone we find our life,
the sun which set that we might rise.

Most Holy God, Word, Spirit: One,
outpoured in love eternally;
you loved us unto death that we
might share your own divinity! Amen.

88.88

41

Lord, find this day acceptable;
with change of heart we turn to you.
On this the day that you have made,
the first love of our hearts renew.

Spring slowly stirs the sleeping earth,
so Easter, too, must take its time.
Rejoice! For Christ has conquered death:
around us all becomes a sign!

O everlasting Trinity,
we would embrace your day of days,
when all creation, fresh, newborn,
will sing its paschal song of praise. Amen.

88.88

Lord God, you claim us for your own in Christ, **42**
and draw us from the dust of mother earth:
be with us on our journey through this Lent,
through deserts to the font of our rebirth.
May fasting leave us hungry for the right,
our alms to others bring some peace and light.

Let us undo the knots that violence ties,
and tear out all that undermines the truth.
Bake bread and feed the hungry till they're full,
and welcome all beneath our ample roof.
Such sacrifice alone gives you delight;
your mercy then will pierce the dark of night.

To fast and feast, there's room enough for each;
so feast, lest from our hearts all joy be stripped.
But let us fast as well, lest feasting blunt
the grave demands of our discipleship.
Soon we will fast and mourn our bridegroom slain;
then, one momentous morning, feast again! Amen.

10.10.10.10.10.10

43

O paradise, O garden of delight,
our dwelling place made perfect by our God,
unending gladness and eternal joy,
the hope of prophets and the home of saints!

The music of your green and rustling leaves
has ever caught our God-Creator's ear,
beseeching that your gates be opened wide,
and all creation now be gathered here.

Let us receive these lenten days with joy,
recalling Eve and Adam's broken fast —
the fruit which parted us from Paradise
but left us longing to return at last.

The Lord, who took our flesh from Mary's womb —
his hour come, for time had run its course —
yearns that the garden thrive and calls to us,
then opens wide its gates upon the cross. Amen.

10.10.10.10

O sun of justice, thaw our hearts;
you draw the spring from earth's decay.
Then melt our safe complacency
which rests content with yesterday.

The "time acceptable" is now!
The dormant earth to growth gives way.
In prayer and fasting thaw our hearts;
let alms a world remade display.

You take us broken as we are,
and spread our dawning days with light;
may we rehearse your ways of love
till all we do gives you delight.

O everlasting Trinity,
we yearn to see that day of days
when all the earth, reborn again,
is vibrant with its Easter praise. Amen.

88.88

45

For forty days Christ fasted, fed
upon the Father's every word —
all for the joy that lay ahead;
such were his pleas, his prayer was heard.

Though one with God he plunged his heart
deep in the world's unfathomed pain;
he wrestled demons, hunger, thirst,
that we in him may do the same.

In Christ our journey is revealed:
his face set toward Jerusalem.
Where he, our head, goes, so must we:
the church, his body, one with him.

O Abba, food of those who fast,
O Christ in whom the least are known,
earth's rising sap, O Spirit-spring:
come raise to life what you have sown! Amen.

88.88

46

O sovereign Christ, creator, Lord,
who yearn we live your living word:
you rush to greet the lost, returned;
your love is given, never earned.

Through wounded hands and feet and side
God calls us: Enter and abide.
The cross you willingly embraced
shows God for us now self-abased.

You who flung forth the star-strewn night
hid in our flesh your dazzling light.
The burdens of our heart you share;
our human cares, our sin, you bear.

Creation trembled once to see
its dying Lord nailed to a tree.
When you cried out your final breath,
the darkened sun so mourned your death.

But now you have been raised on high:
death's conqueror, the crucified!
With robe and ring embrace your own,
and bring us back to our true home. Amen.

88.88

47 Thirty years Christ lived our brother,
servant to the very end.
This his path, he sought no other;
to his passion gave consent.
Crucified before his mother,
hung condemned though innocent.

Soldiers' scorn, the blows, the cruel spit,
slowly crush a human life.
Surely here is bared the limit
of self-hating human strife?
Pierced his side, there flows now from it
living waters, full of life.

Cross of wood, of creatures humblest,
raised above the tallest trees:
yours the fruit from all the forest
plucked to heal our hearts' disease;
awesome wood and nails the noblest,
nobler yet Christ pierced by these.

Bend your branches, tree of splendor;
tend to him whose fate you share.
Let your naked burden's horror
show our hearts betrayed, stripped bare.
You enfold earth's sovereign savior
in these lifeless limbs you bear.

You alone stand contradiction
to our pride or dark despair.
God consumed in crucifixion:
our own life extinguished here.
Partners we in Christ's conviction,
yet, in Christ, are raised co-heirs.

Christ, we worship you and bless you
in your Spirit's bond of peace;
for your cross our earth has made new,
from hell's jaws we gain release.
Abba, Spirit, glory to you
with your Word till ages cease. Amen.

87.87.87

48 Lord, in the desert forty days,
you prayed, from food did fast:
sustain our lenten discipline
to leave behind sin's past.

You met the tempter, and you won;
your prayer your Abba heard.
Give us such openness to trust
in God's life-giving word.

Though parched and hungry, you stood firm,
your heart on God above:
to death's demands let us say no,
but yes to ways of love.

Be with us on our journey, Lord,
throughout these paschal days;
and lead us to the feast of light,
bright Easter's joyous praise. Amen.

86.86

cross,
traced deep
upon your church,
embracing ev'ry
sense and deed:
through you
has Christ
now harrowed hell
and from
its clutches
we are freed.

Holy Triduum

Our Abba had compassion
when Eve and Adam strayed;
when eating fruit forbidden,
death claimed them as its prey.

A second tree God chose then,
more fruitful than before:
God's only son its burden,
whose weight it freely bore.

The cross becomes an altar;
the paschal lamb is killed.
His life-blood for our healing
upon its wood is spilled.

With gall, life's source is fed now;
the thorns and nails and spear
now pierce that noble body,
and water, blood appear.

These flood afresh creation,
the earth and atmosphere,
and bring into its fullness
the church now gathered here. Amen.

76.76

50

Behold the cross, the tree of life
where set the Sun whom we betrayed;
here he in flesh who fleshed our race,
our sentence bore, our ransom paid.

O barren wood, now bloodied, nailed,
you reek of human hate and scorn;
yet from you springs the shoot of life:
a new humanity is born.

O cross, the brand that sears our hearts,
our shame and strength, our ransom price!
This is God's Holy One you bear,
the Lamb, the paschal sacrifice.

O cross, traced deep upon your church,
embracing ev'ry sense and deed:
through you has Christ now harrowed hell
and from its clutches we are freed.

Immortal, holy, mighty God,
whose love for us the spear floods forth:
what love, self-emptied and outpoured,
is here consumed in holocaust.

O Trinity, you stoop to heal
the wounds of earth upon the cross:
all praise be yours as we proclaim
life's glorious rising and its source. Amen.

88.88

51

Behold love's heart, bared by a lance,
the Lamb of God, self-sacrificed!
All who are heavy-burdened, come,
take refuge in the wounds of Christ.

For God's compassion even falls
on those who mock him as he dies,
and Christ assures the dying thief
this day he'll enter Paradise.

Christ lifted high upon the cross
draws to himself all Adam's kin:
in self-abasement, tasting death,
he dies that we may live in him. Amen.

88.88

Rejoice,
O church,
who gave us birth,
the risen Savior
shines on you!
Song through
this holy place resound,
its joyous echoes
earth renew!

Easter Season

Morning during the Octave (1)

We feast this day the death of death,
when heaven's glory harrows hell;
to Christ who did this awesome deed
is raised creation's canticle.

My Christ, they buried me with you,
as yesterday the tomb was sealed;
where we were both conjoined in death —
today your glory is revealed!

Though tears and grief first filled their hearts,
the mourning women mourn no more.
Their gloom is turned to joy in you;
they spread the news: "It is the Lord!"

O victim indestructible,
God's gift so free, love self-effaced,
in rising to your Abba's throne
you raised up Eve and Adam's race.

O Abba, Word and Spirit-spring,
in whom we have been born anew,
our earth is filled with paschal praise:
ours is the joy in hymning you. Amen.

88.88

53

Our justice, Christ, resplendent sun,
from prison tomb bursts forth in light;
within us joy and gladness dance
for Christ is risen in his might.

From death to life we have been raised,
from earth to heaven we are led:
for Christ our resurrection joy
is truly risen as he said.

Let all the heavens burst with joy,
let all the earth with song resound!
Let all creation join the dance
for Christ is risen, death is bound!

Come share the endless reign of Christ;
the hallowed chosen day has come!
Drink freely of the fresh new wine;
there's joy enough for everyone!

O Abba, Word and Spirit-spring
in whom we have been born anew,
our earth is filled with paschal praise;
ours is the joy in hymning you. Amen.

88.88

54

Come one and all, white-robed and washed,
the banquet of the Lamb is spread!
Our exodus is at an end:
proclaim Christ risen from the dead!

For death our blood-stained doors did pass
that night we fled our slavery;
of our oppressors, none survived,
while we passed dry-shod through the sea.

Our Moses, Christ! Our guide, our pasch
whose blood has sanctified us all:
our paschal bread, sincere and true,
whose fragrance fills the wedding hall.

O Word of God, for us enfleshed,
whom we betrayed, for silver sold:
you suffered death, yet loved us still
to give us life a hundredfold.

Hell is no more; its sov'reign head,
deceiving death, is dragged in tow.
You raise us to our Abba's throne,
with all the dead whose names you know.

With boundless love the feast is laid,
yet never did you count the cost!
Our savior, priest and sacrifice —
our shepherd shoulders now the lost! Amen.

88.88

55

With paschal praise be Christ proclaimed,
whose love for us unfolds, astounds:
for by his life-blood we are freed
to live in him beyond death's bounds.

Ours is a paradise undreamed,
whose fruit the tree of life now bears.
Ours is by death's defeat the gift
which Christ-in-us now fully shares.

Ours is the manna here consumed,
bread blessed and broken, shared yet whole!
Ours is the name we each now bear,
breathed deep within our heart and soul.

Ours is the dayspring dawning bright,
whose light now burns within our heart.
Ours is the garment woven white;
yes, ours the very throne of God. Amen.

88.88

56

O God, our light in work or rest,
we bear your image, bright, restored!
In raising Christ from death and grave
you raise us, too, in him, our Lord.

O God, our milk and honey now,
yours is the feast for all to share:
Christ trod the winepress all alone;
the wedding feast is now prepared.

O God, our rainbow, ark, dry land,
whose rage, repented, now is stilled:
Christ, raised, the firstfruits of the dead,
has blessed all earth as you had willed. Amen.

88.88

57

Rejoice, you heavens' mighty powers!
Exult, creation round God's throne!
For Christ our sovereign Lord is raised:
salvation's trumpets make it known!

Rejoice, you earth, resplendent shine,
as radiant you reflect your king!
Christ conquers! Glory covers you!
Night, put to rout, is vanishing!

Rejoice, O church, who gave us birth,
the risen Savior shines on you!
Song through this holy place resound,
its joyous echoes earth renew!

The morning star which never sets
now finds us dazzling as the sun:
Christ, daystar, risen from the dead,
whose radiance rests on everyone! Amen.

88.88

58

The wedding supper of the Lamb,
prepared upon the altar-cross,
awaits us who have shared Christ's pasch
for he has borne its awesome cost.

Christ is to us both host and feast,
unleavened bread and paschal lamb,
the sacrifice forever new,
enthroning us at God's right hand.

We who were not God's people once,
enslaving and enslaved within,
are now the cherished of God's heart
for Christ himself has trampled sin.

In Christ the world's own life lay dead,
yet God this world had loved so well:
that great deceiver's been deceived
and Christ for us has trampled hell.

Sustain, O Abba, this new life
which was in Christ so dearly won.
Accept our sacrifice of praise,
O Abba, Word and Spirit, one. Amen.

88.88

59

As spring buds forth your praise, O Christ,
we too proclaim you, Lord, enthroned:
for in your person we have passed
from exile to our Abba's home.

Compassion for our wintered earth
brings forth a radiant world restored;
flung open is the realm of life
to all whose life proclaims you Lord.

New growth springs up where all seemed dead;
now open is the tomb once sealed.
The stone is rolled away that we
to resurrection life may yield.

With evening here, stay with us, Lord,
that Easter's joy may never end.
In you our world can sing afresh;
in you our earth is sacrament. Amen.

88.88

60

The lenten spring breaks forth today;
it leaves behind an empty cell.
The cross, deep-rooted, bursts in bloom,
proclaiming Christ has harrowed hell.

For neither death's horrendous hold,
nor stone sealed shut before the tomb,
nor guards in vigil, nor death's shroud,
could keep apart the bride and groom.

Amid God's friends, awake with fear,
Christ comes to breathe God's restless peace,
that peace the world can never give:
Christ's gift to us, ours to increase.

O Abba, now in Christ behold
the world as first it came from you:
find in our Easter praise your joy
whereby the earth is made anew. Amen.

88.88

61

O God, in whom the past gives way
from figures to reality:
we stand in awe at what you wrought,
our exodus to liberty.

When Magdalen, distraught, first sees
the teacher of her heart, her friend,
she longs to touch, to cling in love,
but Christ to God must yet ascend.

"Go find my troubled, fearful friends,
and tell them all you've seen and heard."
Apostle to apostles sent,
she first proclaims God's living word.

Upon his friends he breathes new life —
love's wounds emblazon hands and side!
Behold Christ now our Lord and God,
the risen one, the crucified! Amen.

88.88

Christ's is the holy throne of God;
our flesh in Christ is glorified.
Love's open wounds will ever show
the measure of the Crucified.

For Christ is now our plea, our cry,
God's witness to our lives so scarred.
He gathers up, he binds and heals
what seems ignored or spurned or marred.

Content not only to restore,
God graces us with gifts untold:
delight and wonder, courage, joy,
these, soon, God's Spirit will unfold.

Thus your ascension, Lord, proclaims
and draws from us our praise and song.
Our hearts are set where you now dwell:
your Spirit come! For this we long. Amen.

88.88

Exalted on the cross, enthroned,
with death destroyed, Christ journeys home;
while yet withdrawn from human sight
he thrones us at his Abba's right.

Christ's path of passion now comes clear,
no longer clouded by death's fear:
captivity is captive led
and rebels rise in Christ their head!

"Why stand, then, looking heavenward?"
Christ dwells in us, we in the Lord!
Beyond both earth and heav'n above
our lives are hidden in God's love.

In Christ new heavens and new earth
are groaning in the pangs of birth;
their glory soon will be revealed
as with God's Spirit all is sealed!

Exalted, risen, glorious Lord,
one with our God, with God adored!
Your body gathered here in prayer
prays for the Spirit-gift you share! Amen.

88.88

Love of our Abba, love of God the Son,
in whom all things dwell, in whom all are one,
raising new wonders even out of strife:
dwell in us, Spirit! Breathe in us your life!

You, the all-holy, wholly our delight!
Peace is your present; in your presence, light!
Earth, cared and cradled, lies in your embrace:
flame brightly in us! Free us by your grace!

Motherlike, nurt'ring, wise, sincere and just,
truth ever-timeless, source of all our trust!
You touch the human heart — it is enthralled.
Come, Spirit, ravish us. Be all-in-all! Amen.

10.10.10.10

Come now, creating Spirit, come!
Create new worlds and make our hearts
as boundless and as infinite
as is the life your breath imparts!

O gift transcending all we have!
O wondrous, deep, consummate love!
Wellspring of life and searing flame,
our christ'ning into Christ above!

Yours is the open hand of God
whence come new gifts as each has need,
our Abba's promised advocate
when words cannot contain our plea.

Transfuse our every sense with light,
well up in love both bold and pure;
forge us in solidarity
with what the world holds weak and poor.

Through you we know our Abba-God,
through you we know the risen One.
You are their loving, lovely love
at play before all was begun! Amen.

88.88

66

Christ's friends with Mary gather now,
united, one in heart and home;
in prayer they wait the promised gift,
receptive now to God's unknown.

The primal cosmic breath and fire
envelops them with searing pow'r:
creation's birth and Sinai's blaze
both consummated in this hour.

Each one God's holy temple now,
they speak of all they saw and heard;
with new-found tongues they now proclaim
what to the world will seem absurd.

Intoxicated by new wine,
still sober even as they reel,
their former sadness is displaced
by God's own joy, the Spirit's seal!

She forms new hearts and law within,
a new creation fashioning:
have we new eyes, new ways to see
her holiness in everything? Amen.

88.88

67

The many tongues of earth are one
as Babel's curse at last has ceased.
Divisions, hatreds, words of war
are healed in Pentecost's great feast.

O helper, healer of the heart,
come bind earth's wounds, restore the lost.
Then bathed, anointed and refreshed,
we all shall know your Pentecost.

Let every chord on earth now sound,
each voice, each instrument of praise!
Come make of these one fugue of love;
a new humanity now raise! Amen.

88.88

With shadows
death foreshadowing,
now full upon this
fading day,
O Abba, God,
our lives enfold
and keep us safe
in sleep,
we pray.

Night Prayer

With shadows death foreshadowing,
now full upon this fading day,
O Abba, God, our lives enfold
and keep us safe in sleep, we pray.

Those phantom fears which flood the heart
cast out — and dwell more richly there.
Weave dreams, those healing heralds of
your kingdom to which we are heir.

Your glory be a flame this night,
a light to our mortality.
In your embrace we rest secure,
till at the last, your face we see. Amen.

88.88

68

Fast falls the night: stay with us, Lord,
and banish ev'ry care and fear.
When all we trusted fades or fails,
help of the helpless, you are near.

Our lives run swiftly on toward death;
our strength shall ebb, our glory pass.
Let sleep rehearse us night by night
to rest in you, O God, at last.

Come shed the radiance of your cross
upon our closing eyes this night;
then when your endless day has dawned,
death's sleep will yield to boundless light. Amen.

88.88

God-bearing Mother,
whence sprung our Abba's tender love:
light to our darkness,
hope the world despairs of.

With night's unfolding,
gathered once again in Christ's love,
our hearts take up their rest:
our longings and our fears confidently
we take leave of.

Peace-filled, we pray:
you who shared your son's cross,
take to yourself the suff'rings
Christ must still endure—
the sword once spoken of.

Our blessing be in the blessedness
of your hallowed womb:
Jesus, in whom we are new born
to life above.

O loving Mother!
O gentle one!
O tender one!
O Virgin Mary!

TO THE TUNE OF SALVE REGINA

71

O Mary, maiden yet a mother,
daughter of thy Son, beyond all other!
The consummation
planned by God's own decree,
when our lost creation rose in thee!

Mirrored, in thy fashion, is all creation's good:
mercy, might, compassion
grace thy womanhood!

God, who all made, in thy womb was laid:
there God's love was nourished —
warmth which would give increase
to the root whence flourished Christ, our Peace.

TO THE TUNE OF ALMA REDEMPTORIS MATER

72

Woman of deep star-night stillness,
you whom angels claim as their mistress!

Earthen vessel, heaven-bearing:
you the dawn of Christ's appearing!

Woman in the fullest measure,
fallow field of hidden treasure!

Mary, we pray you, be mother:
shelter us in your Son,
Jesus, our brother.

TO THE TUNE OF AVE REGINA CAELORUM

73

Birth-giver of God,
you are graced! Alleluia!

For Christ, the fruit of your womb,
has been raised! Alleluia!

He is risen, and we in him!
Alleluia!

Your blest consent has done this!
Alleluia!

TO THE TUNE OF REGINA COELI

Tones for Ordinary Time

11.11.11.5   Mode VIII

T-19

The Seasonal Tones

*Some of the hymn tones for the seasons are more elaborate than
in Ordinary Time, but they give each season its special identity.
The simpler tones of Ordinary Time may always be substituted for
them, according to meter.*

Advent
Evening

88.88   *Conditor alme siderum:* Mode IV

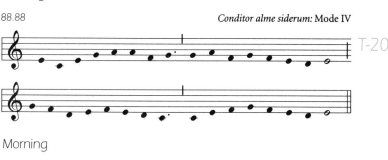

T-20

Morning

88.88   *Vox clara ecce intonat:* Mode IV

T-21

88.88   *Rorate caeli desuper* (adapted): Mode I

T-22

Christmas Season

88.88   The truth from above: Vaughan Williams

T-23

Morning

88.88   *A solis ortus cardine:* Mode III

T-24

Evening

88.88   *Christe redemptor omnium:* Mode I

T-25

Midday

75.75   Mode II (adapted)

T-26

Epiphany Midday

66.86   This Endris Nyght: English, 15th c., adapted

T-27

Lent

88.88   Mode II

T-28

rit.

86.86   Mode II

T-29

Holy Triduum

88.88   Mode II

76.76   *Crux fidelis* (adapted): Mode I

88.88   *Vexilla regis:* Mode I

Easter Season
Morning

88.88   *Aurora lucis rutilat:* Mode VIII

T-34

T-35

T-36

T-37

Evening

88.88   *Ad cenam Agni providi:* Mode VIII

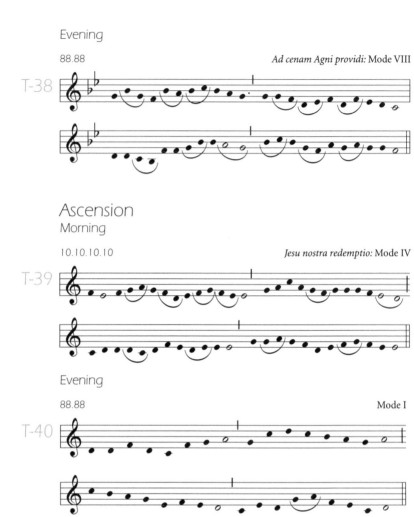

Ascension
Morning

10.10.10.10   *Jesu nostra redemptio:* Mode IV

Evening

88.88   Mode I

Pentecost
Morning

88.88   *Beatus nobis gaudia* (adapted): Mode I

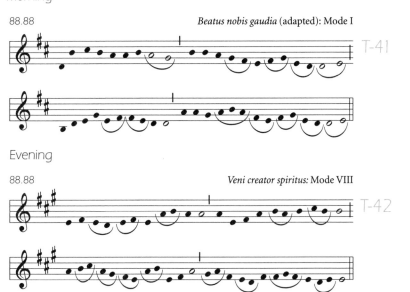

T-41

Evening

88.88   *Veni creator spiritus:* Mode VIII

T-42

Marian Antiphons

Summary and Fall Ordinary Time

Salve Regina: Mode V

God bear-ing Mo-ther, whence sprung our Ab-ba's ten-der love:

light to our dark-ness, hope the world des-pairs of.

With night's un-fold-ing, gath-ered once a-gain in Christ's love,

our hearts take up their rest: our long-ings and our fears,

con - fid - ent - ly we take leave of.

Peace - filled we pray: you who shared your son's cross,

take to your - self the suff'- rings Christ must still en - dure—

the sword once spok - en of. Our bless - ing be

in the bles - sed - ness of your hal - lowed womb: Je - sus

in whom we are new - born to life a - bove. O lov-ing Mo-ther!

O____ ten - der one! O____ gen - tle one! O Vir-gin Mar - y!

Alma redemptoris Mater: Mode V

O___ Ma - ry, maid - en yet a moth - er,

daugh - ter of thy Son, be - yond all oth - er!

The con - sum - mat - ion, planned by God's own de - cree,

when our lost cre - a - tion rose in thee!

Mir - rored, in thy fash - ion,

is all cre - a - tion's good:

mer - cy, might, com - pass - ion grace thy wom - an - hood!

God, who all made, in thy womb was laid:

there God's love was nour - ished—

warmth which would give in - crease

to the root whence flour - ished Christ, our Peace.

The Presentation to Holy Thursday

Ave Regina caelorum: Mode VI

Wo - man of deep star - night still - ness,

you whom an - gels claim as their mis - tress!

Earth - en ves - sel, hea - ven bear - ing;

you, the dawn of Christ's ap - pear - ing!

Wo - man in the ful - lest meas - ure,

fal - low field of hid - den trea - sure!

Ma - ry, we pray you, be mo - ther:

shel - ter us in your son, Je - sus, our bro - ther.

Regina coeli laetare: Mode VI

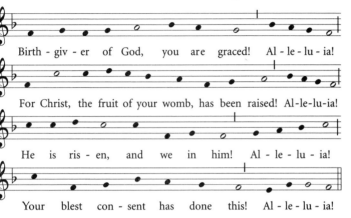

Birth - giv - er of God, you are graced! Al - le - lu - ia!

For Christ, the fruit of your womb, has been raised! Al-le-lu-ia!

He is ris - en, and we in him! Al - le - lu - ia!

Your blest con - sent has done this! Al - le - lu - ia!

Examples of Meters

These familiar hymn tunes may serve as examples of various meters used in this book.

88.88 (Long Meter)

OLD HUNDREDTH. All people that on earth do dwell
ERHALT UNS HERR. Again we keep this solemn fast
ST. CATHERINE. Faith of our fathers
PUER NOBIS. What star is this with beams so bright
EMMANUEL (without refrain)
TALLIS CANON. All praise to thee, my God, this night

66.86 (Short Meter)

SWABIA. 'Tis good, Lord, to be here
SOUTHWELL. Have mercy on us, Lord

86.86 (Common Meter)

LAND OF REST. Jerusalem, my happy home
ANTIOCH. Joy to the world
NEW BRITAIN. Amazing grace

87.87.87

PANGE LINGUA GLORIOSI. *Tantum ergo*
WESTMINSTER ABBEY. Christ is made the sure foundation

87.87

ST. COLUMBA. The king of love my shepherd is
STUTTGART. Come, O long expected Jesus

10.10.10.10

NATIONAL HYMN. God of our fathers
SURSUM CORDA. This world, my God, is held within your hand

11.11.11.5

CHRISTE SANCTORUM. Father, we praise you, now the night is over
BICKFORD. Over the chaos of the empty waters

Further Acknowledgments

Hymn #15 is loosely based on an original Stanbrook Abbey CM text.

Hymn #21 is a free reworking of a Stanbrook Abbey CM hymn.

Hymn #22 is based on the hymn "Strong God, the beam" by Ned O'Gorman, published in *Jubilee*, August 1960.

Hymn #23 is based on the hymn "O true dominion" by Ned O'Gorman, published in *Jubilee*, August 1960.

Hymn #30 is a paraphrase of *Christe redemptor omnium.*

Hymn #33, verses 1–2 alt., Stanbrook Abbey Hymnal.

Hymn #37 is based on a hymn by Hyde W. Beadon, 1812–1891, as published in the Episcopal *Hymnbook 1982,* 138.

Hymn #39 is based on a Stanbrook Abbey composite biblical canticle prose text.

Hymn #42: verse 1 draws on themes from *Catholic Household Blessings and Prayers:* cf. LTP's *Lent Sourcebook,* p. 25. The final verse is freely adapted from themes of the hymn "It shocked them that their master did not fast" by Fred Pratt Green, published in GIA's *Worship III,* 637. Hope Publishing Company, 1982.

Hymn #43 is based on themes drawn from the Byzantine lenten office.

Hymn #46 is loosely based on the hymn "O Christ, our King, Creator" of Gregory the Great in the Lutheran *Book of Worship,* 101.

Hymn #48 is loosely based on "Lord who throughout these forty days" by Claudia Frances Hernaman, 1838–1898, Episcopal *Hymnbook 1982,* 142.

Hymn #49 is a paraphrase of the *Crux fidelis,* loosely based on earlier translations.

Hymns #52 and #53 are a paraphrase of verses of the great Easter canon of Saint John of Damascus.

Hymn #54 is a paraphrase of the *Ad cenam Agni providi.*

Hymn #55 is inspired by the paschal images of the book of Revelation.

Hymn #57 is a paraphrase of the opening of the paschal proclamation.

Hymn #64 is freely adapted from the hymn "Love of the Father," by Robert Bridges, 1844–1930, based on *Amor Patris et Filii,* 12th century.

Hymn #69 was inspired by the hymn "Abide with me" by H. F. Lyte, 1793–1847, as published in the Lutheran *Book of Worship,* 272.

Hymn #71 after a translation of Dante by Ronald Knox.

Doxology #1 is loosely based on an original Stanbrook Abbey CM text.

Index of First Lines

Doxologies

D-1　Most holy God, receive our praise,
together with your Word-made flesh
and holy Wisdom, Three-in-one:
to you we bow, your name we bless. Amen.
88.88

D-2　All praise to you, O Abba, God;
all glory, Christ, beloved Son;
all honor, holy Paraclete.
Proclaim, all creatures, God is one! Amen.
88.88

D-3　We praise you, Christ, beloved Son,
through whom the Holy One is known,
whose Holy Spirit fills the world
and makes in each of us her home. Amen.
88.88

D-4　Forever, Father, with your Word,
together with the Paraclete,
yours be the glory, honor, praise,
till all, in you, shall live complete. Amen.
88.88

D-5　O God, most holy, Three-in-One,
we bow before you filled with praise:
with heaven's host and all that lives
may we adore you all our days. Amen.
88.88